YEAR

WORKING
with
words

Sarah Allen

Contents

Published by
Hopscotch Educational Publishing Ltd,
29 Waterloo Place,
Leamington Spa CV32 5LA
Tel: 01926 744227

© 2001 Hopscotch Educational Publishing

Written by Sarah Allen
Series design by Blade Communications
Illustrated by The Drawing Room
Printed by Clintplan, Southam

ISBN 1-902239-67-9

Sarah Allen hereby asserts her moral right to be identified as the author of this work in accordance with the Copyright, Designs and Patents Act, 1988.

Introduction

About the series

Working with Words is a series of books aimed at developing word skills using story, poetry and non-fiction texts. There is one book for each year group at Key Stage 2.

The series offers a structured approach which provides detailed lesson plans to teach specific word-level skills. Each lesson also contains follow-up ideas to develop sentence- and text-level skills. A unique feature of the series is the provision of differentiated photocopiable activity sheets, where the same activity is presented at three different levels of ability. This helps to reduce teacher-preparation time.

About this book

This book is for teachers of children at Key Stage 2 Year 3 (Scottish level 4). It aims to:

▶ develop children's word-level skills through sharing and discussion of whole-class texts
▶ reinforce the skills and concepts learned in the whole-class session through the use of independent group activities
▶ develop children's sentence- and text-level skills through the provision of a bank of follow-up ideas and activities
▶ support teachers by providing them with stimulating and interesting texts that can be readily copied or enlarged for whole-class use
▶ encourage enjoyment and curiosity as well as develop skills of interpretation and response.

Chapter content

Intended learning

This outlines the word-level learning objectives for the lesson which are matched to The National Literacy Strategy's *Framework for Teaching*.

Starting point: whole class

This section contains two headings: 'Working with the text' and 'Working with words'. 'Working with the text' provides the teacher with suggestions for introducing and using the whole-class text. 'Working with words' contains ideas for developing word-level activities from the text.

Both sections provide samples of questions to ask the children and ideas for developing the skills and concepts being addressed.

Group work

This explains how the three differentiated activity sheets can be used. Guidance is provided for the type of child who will most benefit from each sheet.

Plenary session

This suggests ideas for the whole-class session to discuss the learning outcomes and responses to the activities.

Class text

This is a photocopiable page that can be given to the children or enlarged for whole-class discussion and interpretation.

Sentence-level activities

This contains lots of additional ideas and suggestions for activities to follow up the word-level lesson. The ideas aim to develop sentence-level skills.

Text-level activities

This contains lots of additional ideas and suggestions for activities to follow up the word-level lesson. The ideas aim to develop text-level skills.

Spelling pattern 'le'

Intended learning

▶ To investigate and learn to use the spelling pattern 'le' as in 'little'.

▶ To continue developing dictionary skills.

Starting point: whole class

Working with the text

▶ Explain to the class that this lesson is about words containing the spelling pattern 'le'. Tell the children that they will be looking at a text that comes from a book about bicycles.

▶ Share an enlarged version of the text (or provide each child with their own copy). What does the text tell them about bicycles? Are there some words used that are unfamiliar, such as 'rickshaw' or 'popular'? Ask some of the children to check the meanings of these words in a dictionary.

Working with words

▶ Ask the children if they can see any words containing 'le' in the text. Underline them and list them on the board.

▶ Do they understand the meanings of these words? Write a simple definition next to each 'le' word on the list, preferably a definition provided by the children. Use dictionaries to check these definitions.

▶ Ask them to think of other words with the 'le' spelling pattern. They should not confuse these words with other spelling patterns, such as 'el'. Add the new 'le' words to the list on the board.

▶ The children may notice that the text includes words containing similar-sounding patterns, such as 'bicycle' and 'travel'. Explain that even though the 'el' in 'travel' is pronounced very similarly to the 'le' in 'bicycle', they are in fact different patterns.

▶ When they have grasped the 'le' pattern, move on to the activity sheets. These use 'le' words in other extracts from the book about bicycles.

Group work

Activity sheet 1

This sheet is for less-able children. They have to identify words with the 'le' spelling pattern from a selection of labels on a diagram of a bicycle. They have to put four words into a cloze procedure relating to the bicycle, and think of at least five 'le' words for their own list.

Activity sheet 2

This sheet is for average-ability children. As well as distinguishing the 'le' pattern from words in a different extract about bicycles, they are required to find their own 'le' words.

Activity sheet 3

This sheet is for more-able children. They are given a different extract about bicycles containing more difficult words and should identify those with the 'le' pattern. They solve anagrams of words from the extract and select those with the 'le' pattern. They should identify 'le' words from clues and also find their own words which include this pattern.

Plenary session

▶ Revise the class's understanding of the spelling pattern 'le'. Discuss the activity sheets to identify any difficulties in recognising this pattern. Did they manage to underline all the 'le' words? Did the children working on Activity sheet 3 find it easy or difficult to solve the anagrams? Can they spell all the 'le' words on the activity sheets? Ask some of them to read out the 'le' words that they found for the last part of their activities; add them to the list on the board. Make sure they understand the meanings of the words they suggest.

▶ Look again at the list of 'le' words on the board and ask the class if they can find a way to sort the words, for example in alphabetical order, or grouping rhyming words together.

Sentence-level activities

▶ Using some of the words from the class list, the children could each write six to ten sentences incorporating at least one 'le' word in each sentence. For example, 'At the beach I like to paddle,' and 'Mum is cross when I gobble my trifle.'

▶ For a given period – say a week – challenge the children to find as many sentences as possible in their reading books that contain 'le' words. You could put up a class list against which they could keep a tally for each time they spot a word. They will soon notice which words with this spelling pattern occur most often. The meanings of any new or unusual words should be checked in the dictionary and a definition written next to the word. The sentence in which the word was found could be written out as well.

▶ The same activity, as described above, could be used for words containing the patterns 'el' and/or 'al', so that the differences between the patterns are consolidated.

▶ The children could make up imaginary words containing the 'le' pattern. Start the activity by giving different groups of children real words, such as 'jingle' or 'bangle', and then ask them to make up words to rhyme with these; so they might make a list such as 'jingle', 'fingle', 'ringle', 'dingle' and 'zingle'. Some or all of these words can then be used to make amusing or poetic sentences such as 'Jingle, ringle, zingle went the bells on the horse's harness.' There are many poems that exemplify the use of made-up or nonsense words, such as the works of Edward Lear, particularly 'The Pobble Who Had No Toes' and 'The Runcible Cat'.

▶ Remove the capital letters and/or the full stops from the texts provided on the activity sheets or from the text used in the whole-class starting activity. Provide the children with copies and ask them to insert the missing punctuation in the correct places.

Text-level activities

▶ Read 'The Pobble Who Had No Toes' or 'The Runcible Cat' to the class and ask them to use some of their made-up words as the name for a nonsense character, such as 'The Flingle-Flangle Flea'. They could write a short poem or story about their character using as many 'le' words as possible.

▶ Using the texts provided, suggest that the children identify the gist of the texts, for example by underlining key words or phrases or making notes about two or three main points. They could explain their findings to a partner.

▶ Ask the children to rewrite one of the texts in their own words, using synonyms where appropriate.

▶ Develop the children's library and research skills by asking them to find more information about bicycles or another form of transport. They could make notes about the books they have used, recording the title and author of each book, the chapters and pages where they found the information and a summary of the information. Encourage them to use illustrations and labelled diagrams. The completed work could have an index, contents page, glossary and so on.

▶ Using their existing knowledge and their imaginations, the children could invent their own modes of transport for a specific purpose, such as looking for the Loch Ness monster or for travelling through space or through time. They could draw and label their device and write a passage about it describing the fuel it uses, how it moves, its gizmos and attachments and so on. These could be collected in a book or used as a wall display.

All about bicycles

Apart from walking, cycling is the easiest and cheapest way to travel. The bicycle is one of the few vehicles that does not cause pollution because the only fuel it needs is the energy provided by the legs of its rider!

The bicycle is very popular in countries such as China and India. A common form of public transport in these countries is the rickshaw, which is a small carriage for one or sometimes two people attached to a bicycle, and driven purely by the muscle power of the cyclist.

Some bicycles carry baskets fixed with strong straps and buckles to the handlebars. These can be used by shopkeepers for delivering goods to their customers, and were a common sight in Britain during the early to mid 20th century. A bicycle can also be attached to a cold box, and this was an early form of ice-cream van known as a 'Stop Me and Buy One', popular before the development of refrigerated vehicles.

Tricycles are cycles with three wheels. These cycles are easier for young children to handle.

Today, mountain bikes make it possible for cyclists to scramble over all kinds of terrain from humble bumps to huge mountains!

All about bicycles

1. Here is a diagram of a bicycle with various parts labelled. Underline every word that has the 'le' spelling pattern.

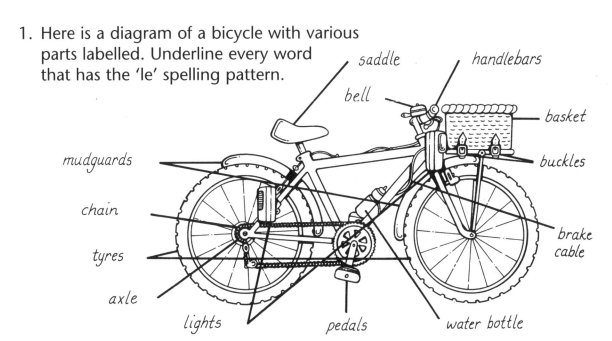

saddle   handlebars

bell

basket

mudguards

buckles

chain

tyres

brake cable

axle

lights   pedals   water bottle

2. Now choose the correct words from the box to complete these sentences. The first one has been done for you.

A bicycle is a <u>vehicle</u> that does not cause pollution.

When you ride a bike you sit on the _____

A bell can be fixed to the _____

A three-wheeled bicycle is called a _____

The basket is fixed on with _____

tricycle
table
buckles
vehicle
saddle
bicycle
paddle
handlebars
triangle
candle

3. Use a dictionary to help you find more words that contain the spelling pattern 'le'. One has been done for you.

a) _tumble_____   d) _____

b) _____   e) _____

c) _____   f) _____

4. If you can find more, write them on the back of this sheet.

All about bicycles

1. Here is some text from an information book about bicycles.
   Read it carefully and then underline at least five words that contain
   the 'le' pattern. One has been done for you. Use a dictionary to check
   the meanings of any words you don't know.

> There are <u>cycles</u> for every need – tricycles for toddlers,
> tandems for two riders and the unicycle for circus artistes, as
> well as the ordinary bicycle. Bikes can travel where many
> other kinds of vehicle cannot. The sturdy mountain bike with
> its wide tyres and strong light frame is suitable for even the
> most difficult ground. If you want more speed, many types of
> motorcycle are available. However, these need more
> maintenance, as well as fuel, so are more expensive.

2. Now draw lines to match the words with the same spelling pattern.
   Then find one more 'le' word to go with each pair. The first one has
   been done for you.

dangle	cattle	rattle
cuddle	winkle	_____
rumble	riddle	_____
cable	kettle	_____
middle	tangle	_____
battle	tumble	_____
nettle	muddle	_____
tinkle	stable	_____

3. If you can find more, write them on the back of this sheet.

All about bicycles

1. Here is some text from an information book about bicycles.
   Read it carefully and then underline at least six words that
   contain the 'le' pattern.

A modern bicycle is small and lightweight, easily manoeuvrable and
therefore perfect for use in both town and country. However, early bicycles
were very different. The bicycle was invented in 1790 by a French
nobleman, the Comte de Sivrac, and was made from wood. Other designs
soon followed. These had solid tyres of metal and a hard saddle, and so were
very uncomfortable to ride. One of the earliest was called the hobby-horse,
and the rider simply walked along astride the cycle, as there were no pedals
to propel it. The penny-farthing was a very tall bicycle, with a huge wheel
at the front and a little one behind. It was difficult to mount and it was only
possible to ride it safely after long practice. It needed much skill and balance
because it was so unstable. Many of the early designs of bicycle were known
as boneshakers, because they gave their owners such a rough ride.

2. Untangle these anagrams to make words from the extract above.
   Then underline those that have the 'le' spelling pattern.

   cybicle   latem   dadles   slaped   yelsaf   lettil   kwedal   blessiop   stunbale

3. Which 'le' words are needed to complete these sentences?

   Tarzan and Jane live in the _____

   A stinging plant is a _____

   To protect your eyes when swimming you wear _____

   A fight between two armies is a_____

   Another name for a violin is a _____

   If there is a power cut you might need a _____

   To protect your finger when sewing you need a _____

4. How many more 'le' words can you think of? Write them on the back
   of this sheet.

Inferring meaning

Intended learning

▶ To infer the meaning of unknown words from context.

▶ To recognise that inference may not produce exact meanings, but that meanings inferred should be based on sensible deductions from the information available.

Starting point: whole class

Working with the text

▶ Explain that this lesson is about how to work out the meanings of words. Ask the children what they do when they come across a word they don't know. Discuss the different strategies used and explain the meaning of the term 'inference'. Tell them that they are going to look at a poem that contains words they may not know.

▶ Read 'The Bogeyman' to the class in such a way that the general meaning is conveyed but without dwelling on the unusual words. What do they think of the poem? What is a bogeyman?

▶ Read the poem again, but this time more slowly (use an enlarged version of the poem so that the children can see the words). Ask them to look for any unfamiliar words and to think about the scene the poet sets.

Working with words

▶ Ask the children to look at the first verse. Underline any unfamiliar words they have noticed and list them. Ask them how they might be able to work out the meanings. For example, for 'In the desolate depths of a perilous place' talk about the kind of place in which a bogeyman would be found – is a 'perilous place' likely to be safe or dangerous? Remind the children that to infer a meaning, they should read to the end of the line(s) to get the gist of the passage and then go back to the unknown word(s).

▶ Continue looking at unfamiliar words in the rest of the poem. The children may recognise some words but not fully understand their meanings. This is where the importance of context can be emphasised;

the children should recognise that the suggested meanings must fit in with the rest of the poem. For example, in verse two the word 'skulks' may be unknown, but by looking at the whole verse it becomes clear that the bogeyman wants to catch a child and that there are shadows; thus a good assumption would be that the bogeyman is hiding.

▶ Write the possible meanings next to the words/phrases on the list. Ask the children to use dictionaries to look up the meanings of the words. How close were their guesses?

▶ Explain that knowing the meanings of the words can help us to read the poem with more expression. Invite the children to read out some of the lines with expression. Do they enjoy the poem more now that the meanings are clearer?

Group work

Activity sheet 1

This sheet is for less-able children. They are required to infer meanings for words from a poem extract and a set of unrelated sentences. They are given word lists for support.

Activity sheet 2

This sheet is for children who still need some guidance in making inferences.

Activity sheet 3

This sheet is for more-able children. They are given less support.

Plenary session

▶ Share the activity sheet work. Did the children have any problems making inferences? How close were their inferences to the dictionary definitions?

▶ Why do the children think authors and poets use 'difficult' words rather than 'easy' ones ('hilarious' rather than 'funny')? Explain how important it is to have several words with the same or similar meaning, in order to make language more interesting both to read and to listen to.

Sentence-level activities

▶ Use some of the sentences from 'The Bogeyman' and the activity sheet poems to study the impact of the verbs chosen by the poets. Ask the children to substitute verbs with similar meanings to see what effect these have. Can they 'improve' the poems using their own words?

▶ Working with extracts from 'The Bogeyman' and the activity sheet poems, consider the purpose of the punctuation. What would be the effect on meaning if the question marks, exclamation marks, dashes and ellipses were omitted? Could they be replaced with another type of punctuation?

▶ Give the children sentences written as statements and ask them to rewrite them as questions with the correct punctuation. For example, 'The bogeyman skulks in the shadows,' could become 'Does the bogeyman skulk in the shadows?'

▶ Challenge them to classify the verbs from 'The Bogeyman' and the activity sheet poems into groups, for example 'stalk'/'pad'/'rear'/'thresh' and 'lurks'/'waiting'/'skulks'. This activity could be done in pairs or small groups. Ask the children to add to these groups of verbs by finding verbs with similar meanings in the dictionary or their general reading activities.

▶ 'The Bogeyman' and the activity sheet poems are written mainly in the present tense. Why might the poets have chosen to do this? Does the present tense have more impact? How? Can the children rewrite parts of the poems in the past or future tenses? Is this easy/difficult? What is the effect? Do the texts still make sense? Are they more or less interesting or amusing?

Text-level activities

▶ Ask the children to write the story of 'The Bogeyman', using some of the vocabulary in the poem. Challenge them to write as vividly and imaginatively as possible, using suitable verbs and adjectives.

▶ Ask them to conduct comparisons between the original poem and their new prose versions of the monster. Which do they prefer? Why? Which version sounds best or is more interesting?

▶ Provide copies of poems containing made-up words, such as 'Jabberwocky' by Lewis Carroll. They should make inferences as to the meanings of words like 'brillig' and 'slithy', and then produce their own prose versions of the poem, using their 'translations' of Carroll's language. The advantage here is that there are no definitive meanings available for the made-up words.

▶ A variation on the above suggestion is for the children to make up their own words and use them to describe imaginary monsters. Remind them that not all monsters are bad. They should consider what their new monsters look like, how they move, what they eat, where they live, what noises they make, what they are called and so on. Further inspiration can be found in the Greek myths. *Monster Poems* by John Foster and Korky Paul (OUP 1995) has more monster poems and illustrations.

▶ Challenge the children to produce Monster Dialogues. Ask them to imagine the conversation that takes place as the monsters meet. The dialogue could be performed to the rest of the class, recorded on cassette or made into a book.

The Bogeyman

In the desolate depths of a perilous place
the bogeyman lurks, with a snarl on his face.
Never dare, never dare to approach his dark lair
for he's waiting…just waiting…to get you.

He skulks in the shadows, relentless and wild
in his search for a tender, delectable child.
With his steely sharp claws and his slavering jaws
oh he's waiting…just waiting…to get you.

Many have entered his dreary domain
but not even one has been heard from again.
They no doubt make a feast for the butchering beast
and he's waiting…just waiting…to get you.

In that sulphurous, sunless and sinister place
he'll crumple your bones in his bogey embrace.
Never never go near if you hold your life dear,
for oh!…what he'll do…when he gets you!

Jack Prelutsky

Sasquatch

1. Read the text below. Draw a line from each underlined word to the one in the lists that you think means the same. The first one has been done for you.

stalk:
walk about
creep secretly
hide
watch

timberland:
forest
planks
branches
countryside

cabins:
cupboards
houses
piles
huts

I stalk the timberland,
I wreck and splinter through,
I smash log cabins,
I wrestle grizzly bears.
At lunch-time if I'm dry
I drain a lake or two,
I send the wolves and wolverines
Howling to their lairs.
I'm Sasquatch,
Bigfoot,
Call me what you like,
But if you're a backpacker
On a forest hike,
Keep a watch behind you,
I'm there, though rarely seen.
I'm Bigfoot,
Sasquatch,
I'm mean, mean, mean.

lairs:
cubs
dens
mates
stars

Sasquatch:
hungry
a hairy monster
tall
small

hike:
walk
log camp
bike

2. Now infer the meanings of the underlined words in these sentences. The words in the box might help you.
Don't look in the dictionary until you have finished!

The runner passed the baton to the next person.

Dennis the Menace and Gnasher are rascals.

Tom was excited to be going to the football stadium.

Superman had a plot to save the people.

bomb
mask
stick
plan
ground
naughty
arena
angels
match
saddle
scamps
game

3. Now check your answers in the dictionary or thesaurus. Were you right?

Yeti

1. Read the poem below. Draw a line from each underlined word to the one in the list that you think means the same. The first one has been done for you.

ski
ghost
whirlwind
countryside
signpost
doze
hateful
walk quietly
alien
jump
hillside
road
climb
snowstorm
cuddly
ice-field
fly
spirit

I pad across the snow field,
Silent as a thief,
The phantom of the blizzard,
Vanishy, rare.
I haunt the barren glacier
And men in disbelief
Goggle at the footprints
I scatter here and there.
I'm Abominable,
Yeti,
Call me what you choose,
But if you're a mountaineer,
Careful when you snooze,
I'm the restless roaming spirit
Of the Himalayan range.
I'm Yeti,
Abominable,
I'm strange, strange, strange.

2. Now infer the meanings of the underlined words in these sentences and write them in the spaces. When you have finished look in the dictionary to see if you were right.

We had a real feast at the wedding banquet. _____

The trunk of the tree was very gnarled. _____

Our school is getting a temporary hall while the new one is being built.

_____

I went to the optician to get new glasses. _____

The little girl hid behind the chair because she was bashful.

_____

Nessie

1. Read the poem below. Use clues from the poem to think of a meaning for each underlined word. Write your meanings in the spaces. One has been done for you.

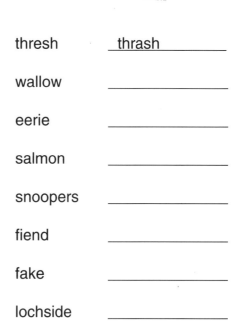

I rear up from the waves,
I <u>thresh</u>, I <u>wallow</u>,
My seven snaky humps
Leave an <u>eerie</u> wake.
I crunch the silly <u>salmon</u>,
Twenty at one swallow,
I tease the silly <u>snoopers</u> –
A <u>fiend</u>? A fish? A <u>fake</u>?
I'm the Monster,
Nessie,
Call me what you please,
But if you're a camper
In the <u>lochside</u> trees,
Before you zip your tent at night
Say your prayers and kneel.
I'm Nessie,
The Monster,
I'm real, real, real.

thresh	thrash
wallow	
eerie	
salmon	
snoopers	
fiend	
fake	
lochside	

2. Now infer the meaning of the underlined words in these sentences. Each meaning can be a word or a phrase. Write your meanings on the back of this sheet. When you have finished look in the dictionary to check whether you were right.

The <u>vegetation</u> in the jungle is very thick and green.

The <u>population</u> of New Town is 2000.

It is more <u>convenient</u> to go to our local shop rather than the supermarket.

We studied the <u>inscriptions</u> on the gravestones.

In PE we sometimes use the mats and <u>apparatus</u>.

At the circus Beppo and Jojo the clowns were <u>hilarious</u>.

CHAPTER THREE

Spelling by analogy

Intended learning

▶ To use independent spelling strategies, namely: spelling by analogy with other known words, for example 'light' and 'fright'.

▶ To continue developing dictionary skills.

Starting point: whole class

Working with the text

▶ Tell the children that this lesson is going to help them with their spelling. Explain that they are going to use words that they can already spell to help them learn how to spell other words. Tell them that this is called spelling by analogy.

▶ Give them an example, such as the word 'can'. Show them that if they are able to spell 'can', they can also spell 'Dan', 'fan', 'Gran', 'man', 'Nan', 'pan' and so on. Write these words on the board and underline the letters 'an' so that they can begin to see the patterns in the lists of analogous words. Emphasise that they are looking at the same letter pattern and not necessarily the sound the letters make, otherwise the children may conclude that all words that rhyme have the same letter patterns.

▶ Share an enlarged version of the text with the children. What kind of story is it? What other traditional tales do they know?

Working with words

▶ Write the following words from the text on the board: 'light', 'nightie', 'right' and 'fright'. Can the children see which parts of these words are spelled the same? Underline the 'ight' in each word. Can they spell other words using this same pattern? Challenge them to spell words such as 'bright', 'might' and 'sight'.

▶ Repeat the activity with other words from the story, such as 'jolly' – 'holly', 'dolly', 'folly', 'golly', 'lolly', 'Molly', 'Polly'; and 'quick' – 'trick', 'brick', 'click', 'flick', 'kick'. Spellings and meanings should be checked using a dictionary where appropriate.

▶ Tell the children that they are going to look at another traditional story to find words that have the same spelling pattern.

Group work

Activity sheet 1

This sheet is suitable for children who need a higher degree of guidance in following instructions and/or are less confident readers and writers. They have to find analogies for given words, using the initial letter sounds provided to help them. They are also asked to look up the meanings of four other analogous words in a dictionary. They are given a suggestion for making their own list of analogies for the word 'three'.

Activity sheet 2

This sheet is aimed at children who can work with confidence but still need some guidance. They are asked to find analogies for each of four given words, choosing from a list. They then have to find words that fit the meanings provided, making an analogy with a given clue word. It is suggested they make their own list of analogies for the word 'chin'.

Activity sheet 3

Children working on this sheet will be confident, independent readers and writers, able to follow more complex instructions. They have to find at least six analogies for given words, using their own knowledge and a dictionary if necessary. As on Activity sheet 2, they are asked to find words that fit the meanings provided but on this sheet the words are more challenging. It is suggested they make their own list of analogies for the word 'tried'.

Plenary session

▶ Bring the children together and revise their understanding of the term 'analogy' by discussing the work on the activity sheets. Which words did they have problems with? How do they think learning about analogies will help them with their spelling?

Sentence-level activities

▶ Use 'Little Red Riding Hood' to explore the function of adjectives. Ask the children to identify the adjectives in the story. They could then experiment with deleting and substituting the adjectives to consider the effect this has on meaning. They could also use thesauruses to find more powerful or descriptive adjectives to describe the wolf, granny and the wood-cutter.

▶ Have fun exploring plurals by asking the children to make up counting sentences about characters in traditional tales. For example, 'One big bad wolf', 'Two lost children' (Hansel and Gretel), 'Three little pigs' and 'Seven lively dwarfs'.

▶ Look at the use of capitalisation in the story to show emphasis. What does this tell the reader? Challenge the children to write some sentences where particular words need emphasis. They could act them out.

▶ Provide copies of the extracts from either of the two stories with some of the punctuation missing, such as capital letters, full stops, or exclamation, question and speech marks. Challenge the children to put in the correct punctuation.

▶ Use the two extracts or any other suitable familiar tales, for work on speech marks, dialogue and paragraphs. You could remove the paragraph breaks to demonstrate that texts are more difficult to read and understand when they are not separated by paragraph breaks.

Text-level activities

▶ Ask the children to write character portraits of the characters in 'Little Red Riding Hood'. The more-able could be challenged to write non-stereotypical ones, for example a portrait of the wolf who isn't really bad but has just been misunderstood!

▶ Collect different versions of traditional stories, make comparisons and decide which versions are best. Consider versions such as *Revolting Rhymes* by Roald Dahl as well as traditional fairytale books. The children could compare beginnings and endings, the events and characters and also the dialogue. They could look at the authors' choice of verbs and/or adjectives and how these affect the atmosphere created. Which version has the most impact? Why?

▶ Following the above activity, ask the children to write their own versions of a favourite story, trying to make it as interesting as possible for the reader, for example by including the most exciting descriptions or most amusing dialogue. These could be used as a class reading resource.

▶ Ask the children to collect opening sentences from other well-known stories, either from memory or by looking at the actual texts. Then ask them to make suggestions for improving the opening sentences for the stories of 'The Three Little Pigs' and 'Little Red Riding Hood' used in the lesson. They could do the same with closing sentences and then write their own versions of suitable endings for these stories and others.

Little Red Riding Hood

Little Red Riding Hood's mum sent Little Red Riding Hood off with a light basket of goodies to visit Granny, who lived alone in a cottage in the woods.

As she skipped along the path, the big bad wolf saw her and asked, 'Where are you off to this fine day, Little Red Riding Hood?'

'I'm taking this basket of goodies to my Granny, who's ill in bed,' Little Red Riding Hood replied.

Now, not only was the wolf big and bad, he was also very crafty, and when he heard this, he had an idea for a jolly good feed. He ran ahead of Little Red Riding Hood, and reached Granny's house in a jiffy. The door was ajar, so he crept in, and before she knew it, he had grabbed Granny in his big strong jaws and gobbled her up whole! He dressed himself in Granny's nightie double quick and jumped into her bed just as Little Red Riding Hood knocked at the door.

Little Red Riding Hood went up to the bed to give Granny a kiss. 'Granny must be feeling very poorly,' she thought. 'Something's not right; she looks such a fright!'

Aloud she said, 'What big ears you have, Granny!'

'All the better to hear you with, my dear,' replied Granny wolf.

'And what big eyes you have, Granny!' said Little Red Riding Hood.

'All the better to see you with, my dear,' answered Granny wolf.

'And what big TEETH you have, Granny!' exclaimed Little Red Riding Hood.

'All the better to EAT YOU WITH!' snarled Granny wolf, and quick as a flash the wolf grabbed Little Red Riding Hood in his big strong jaws and gobbled her up whole!

Luckily, a wood-cutter had seen the wolf enter the cottage, and he rushed in just as the wolf was licking his drooling lips. Quick as a wink, he drew his axe and chopped off the wolf's head before the wolf knew what was happening. Then he opened the wolf's tummy and out stepped Granny and Little Red Riding Hood, none the worse for their adventure.

But forever afterwards, they were both very suspicious of people with large teeth!

The Three Little Pigs

1. Here is an extract from 'The Three Little Pigs'.
   Read it carefully and then follow the instructions.

> The first little <u>pig</u> <u>went</u> on his <u>way</u> and met a
> <u>man</u> carrying a bale of straw. 'Please let me have
> some straw to build my house,' said the first little
> pig. The man agreed, and the little pig built
> himself a house of straw.

2. Use these words from the story to make more words that have
   the same spelling pattern. The first one has been done for you.

pig	went	way	man
dig___	b_____	h_____	f_____
b_____	d_____	pl_____	p_____
w_____	t_____	r_____	v_____

3. Now find the words below in the dictionary and write their meanings
   in the spaces provided.

   twig _____

   rent _____

   bay _____

   tan _____

4. On the back of this sheet list all the words you can find that have the same
   spelling pattern as the word 'three'. (Hint: here's the first – 'bee'.)

The Three Little Pigs

1. Read this extract from 'The Three Little Pigs'. Then follow the instructions.

<u>Soon</u> a big bad wolf came by the first little pig's <u>house</u> of straw. He was feeling very hungry. 'Little pig, little pig, let me come in or I will huff and puff and <u>blow</u> your house down!' cried the wolf. 'No, no!' replied the little pig. 'By the <u>hair</u> of my chinny-chin-chin, I'll not let you in!' So the big bad wolf huffed and he puffed and he blew down the house of straw and gobbled up the first little pig.

2. The words in the boxes below are all from the story. Add more words that have the same spelling patterns. One has been done for you. Use the word box below to help you.

soon	**house**	**blow**	**hair**
moon			

> balloon   stair   slow   mouse   drew   town   spoon   flew   crown
> fair   crow   louse   air   moon   throw   knew   clown   grouse

3. Complete these sentences. The words in brackets are clues; they have the same spelling patterns as the missing words. The first one has been done for you.

A word meaning a husband or a wife is _spouse_. (house)

A word meaning midday is _____ (soon)

Another word for a very special dress is _____ (down)

To shine brightly is to _____ (blow)

The den of a wild animal is its _____ (hair)

Vegetables cooked together are a _____ (blew)

4. On the back of this sheet list all the words you can find that have the same spelling pattern as the word 'chin'.

The Three Little Pigs

1. Here is an extract from 'The Three Little Pigs'. Read it carefully and then follow the instructions.

> At last the big bad wolf reached the third little pig's house of bricks. He wasn't hungry any more, but being a greedy wolf he roared, 'Little pig, little pig, let me come in or I will huff and puff and blow your house down!' 'No, no!' the little pig yelled back. 'By the hair of my chinny-chin-chin I'll not let you in!' So the big bad wolf huffed and puffed, and he huffed and he puffed, but no matter how hard he tried he couldn't blow down the house of bricks. Inside, the clever third little pig, who was not at all afraid, boiled up some water in a big pot on his fire. Outside, the big bad wolf climbed onto the roof in order to go down the chimney to get the little pig. The wolf started to climb down the chimney when suddenly he fell, and landed in the pot with a SPLASH! Before he knew it, he was boiled and the third little pig was gobbling him up!

2. Find at least six words with the same spelling pattern as each of these words from the extract above. Write your answers on another sheet of paper. You can use a dictionary to help you.

bricks	greedy	back	splash

3. Complete these sentences. The words in the brackets are clues; they have the same spelling patterns as the missing words. You can use a dictionary.

To travel somewhere new to make discoveries is to <u>explore</u>. (more)

Children need a good diet in order to _____ properly. (blow)

To talk idly and rapidly is to _____ (matter)

The middle of an apple where the pips are is the _____ (more)

Another name for a church steeple is a _____ (fire)

Snails, tortoises and oysters all live in a _____ (fell)

To ruin something is to _____ it. (boil)

4. On the back of this sheet list all the words you can find that have the same spelling pattern as the word 'tried'.

Compound words

CHAPTER FOUR

Intended learning

▶ To recognise and generate compound words and to use this knowledge to support spelling.

Starting point: whole class

Working with the text

▶ Tell the children that they are going to perform a poem from Jamaica called 'Barefoot'. Provide them with their own copy of the poem (or enlarge it). Read the poem to the children first, asking them to follow the words as you read. Use this reading to model how the words in the poem could be expressed or performed.

▶ What do the children notice about the spelling of some of the words in the poem? Does this tell us how the words should be spoken out loud? Why is it written like this? Does it give the reader a feel for the way some Jamaicans might speak? Do they like the poem? Why/why not? What is it trying to tell us? Do they think the poet likes going barefoot? What warning is he giving us?

▶ Tell the children that they are now going to perform the poem themselves. Divide the class into two groups. One group is to say the chorus ('Inna yuh barefoot') and the other group is to say the action lines. They could stand up in lines and face each other to perform the poem. Encourage them to keep an even pace in order to keep the rhythm of the poem going.

Working with words

▶ Sit the children down again and write the title of the poem on the board. Do they notice anything about the word? Discuss the fact that the word is actually made up of two smaller words and explain that this type of word is called 'compound'.

▶ Can the children think of any other compound words to do with the body? Give them a few to start with, such as armpit, headache and eyelash. List all their words on the board and ask them to look through the poem – can they find any other compound words? Add these to the list.

▶ Divide the children into pairs. Ask them to play a game where one person says the beginning of a compound word and their partner has to think of a suitable ending, for example 'play' + 'time', 'tooth' + 'ache'. How many different compound words can they make? Share the responses and add any new ones to the list on the board.

▶ Explain that splitting a compound word into two or more separate words can help when trying to spell the whole word. Once we know how to spell the base word of a compound word this helps us to spell other words with this base. Explain that the base word can be at the beginning (bookmark) or end (notebook). Knowing how to spell 'ache' can help us to spell 'headache' and 'toothache'.

▶ Tell the children that they are now going to explore compound words further.

Group work

Activity sheet 1

This sheet is intended for children who need more support. They are required to match words to make compound words and use a dictionary to find definitions for the new words.

Activity sheet 2

This sheet is aimed at more confident readers. The tasks are more demanding than on Activity sheet 1 but a degree of support is included in the form of an example. They are required to write definitions for five of their words.

Activity sheet 3

This sheet is aimed at independent readers and writers. They should use a dictionary to generate their own compound words and to write the definitions for five of these.

Plenary session

▶ Revise understanding of the term 'compound word' by sharing the activity sheet work. What was the most interesting or surprising word found? Add the children's words to the list from the starter session.

Sentence-level activities

▶ Using the class list of compound words already generated, ask each child to make up a few sentences, that incorporate at least one of the words from the list. They could write them down or just say them.

▶ Provide the children with one or two sentences containing at least one word that can be made into compounds. Ask them to identify the word and list the possible compounds, which they then incorporate into new sentences. For example, a starting sentence might be 'It was a wonderful place for a child to play.' The children could then identify 'child' or 'play' (or both) and produce a few sentences containing compounds of these words.

▶ Using some of the words/sentences from the activity sheets and subsequent work, the children could consolidate their understanding of plurals. Provide sentences in the singular which incorporate parts of the body, such as 'The boy had to wash his dirty foot.' The task is to rewrite the sentences in the plural, so the sentence above would become 'The boys had to wash their dirty feet.' The activity can be reversed, so that a plural sentence needs to be converted to the singular.

▶ Explore verbs by using the poem as a starting point. How many different ways can you move your feet? Challenge the children to write interesting sentences, perhaps using alliteration, for example 'I can twist, turn, tickle, tumble, tangle, tap, tense and twitch my toes.'

▶ Explore adjectives by asking the children to think of suitable descriptive words to qualify the word 'barefoot' in the poem, for example 'inna yuh wonderful barefoot', 'inna yuh silky barefoot'. They can make up new sentences for the poem in this way.

Text-level activities

▶ Ask the children to look for more performance poems from other cultures. They could perform these poems for other classes.

▶ Ask the children to carry out research into the body. They could create a class instruction manual on aspects of body care. They could investigate issues such as personal hygiene, for example how to wash hands or clean teeth correctly. Each child could then produce a detailed set of instructions for performing the activity, with diagrams if appropriate. When complete, the instructions could be swapped around and comments made on whether they are effective or not. Are the instructions clear and easy to follow? Is there enough or too much detail? Will the instructions work? Are the diagrams helpful?

▶ The above activity could be repeated, this time for someone who does not speak English or cannot read, like a younger child or even an alien from another world. How will this affect the way they give their instructions (diagrams only, for example)? Does this make the task easier or harder? Inspiration for this task may be found in books such as the *Dr. Xargle* series by Jeanne Willis and Tony Ross.

▶ Challenge the children to write new or extended verses for the poem 'Barefoot'. What else can they do in their bare feet? Add appropriate lines to the poem.

Barefoot

Yuh can jump
  Inna yuh barefoot!
Yuh can run
  Inna yuh barefoot!
Yuh can walk strong
  Inna yuh barefoot!
Yuh can walk near
  Inna yuh barefoot!
Yuh can walk far
  Inna yuh barefoot!
Yuh can guh a markit
  Inna yuh barefoot!
Yuh can guh a riva
  Inna yuh barefoot!
Yuh can guh a sea
  Inna yuh barefoot!
Yuh can pray
  Inna yuh barefoot!
Yuh can dance
  Inna yuh barefoot!
Yuh can rap
  Inna yuh barefoot!
Yuh can guh a skool
  Inna yuh barefoot!
Yuh feel free
  Inna yuh barefoot!
Yuh feel good
  Inna yuh barefoot!
Yuh feel ire
  Inna yuh barefoot!
Yuh can climb coconut tree
  Inna yuh barefoot!

Yuh can kick a football
  Inna yuh barefoot!
De sun nice
  Inna yuh barefoot!
De rain sweet
  Inna yuh barefoot!
Yuh skin tuff
  Inna yuh barefoot!
Yuh toes ruff
  Inna yuh barefoot!

But!
If yuh mash up yuh toes
  Inna yuh barefoot!
Get a cut
  Inna yuh barefoot!
Yuh cyaan walk
  Inna yuh barefoot!
So step cool
  Inna yuh barefoot!
Doan ac' fool
  Inna yuh barefoot!
Ah yuh will always walk
  Inna yuh barefoot!
Jus cool
  Inna yuh barefoot!
Jus nice
  Inna yuh barefoot!
Yuh can do anyting
  Inna yuh barefoot!

Martin Glynn

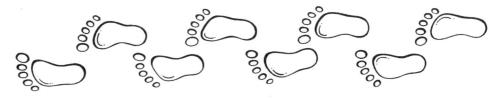

Compound words

1. Here is an extract from 'Barefoot' by Martin Glynn.

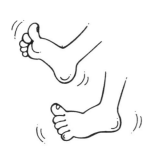

> Yuh can guh a sea
> > Inna yuh barefoot!
> Yuh can pray
> > Inna yuh barefoot!
> Yuh can dance
> > Inna yuh barefoot!
> Yuh can rap
> > Inna yuh barefoot!
> Yuh can guh a skool
> > Inna yuh barefoot!
> Yuh feel free
> > Inna yuh barefoot!

2. Match these words from the poem to a word from the list below to make new compound words. One has been done for you.

sea	**school (skool)**	**free**
sea + side = seaside		

side	teacher	wheel	shore	house	style

3. Now make some compound words by filling in the gaps with words from the box below. The first one shows you how.

hand<u>shake</u>   hand_____   finger_____   wrist_____

print	nail	stand	bag	cuff	watch	shake

4. See how many more compound words you can make that use parts of the body. Write them on the back of this sheet. Find definitions for them. Use a dictionary to help you.

Compound words

1. Here is an extract from 'Barefoot' by Martin Glynn.

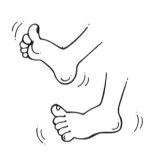

> Yuh can jump
>   Inna yuh barefoot!
> Yuh can <u>run</u>
>   Inna yuh barefoot!
> Yuh can walk <u>strong</u>
>   Inna yuh barefoot!
> Yuh can walk <u>near</u>
>   Inna yuh barefoot!
> Yuh can walk <u>far</u>
>   Inna yuh barefoot!

2. Add words from the box below to the underlined words in the poem to make new compound words. Use a dictionary to help you. One has been done for you.

   <u>strongbox</u>   _____   _____

   _____   _____   _____

side	about	hold	away	box	by	room

3. Use some of the words below to make at least ten compound words. Write them on the back of this sheet. You can use each word more than once if you need to.

arm	hand	wrist	finger	knee	foot
toe	body	stomach	made	ache	rest
nail	hole	band	shake	print	cap
	tip	step	ball	guard	

4. Now use a dictionary to check that the words you have made are real words. Choose five of your compound words and find definitions for them. Write the definitions on the back of this sheet.

Compound words

1. Here is an extract from 'Barefoot' by Martin Glynn.

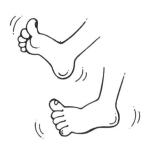

> But!
> If yuh mash up yuh toes
>   Inna yuh barefoot!
> Get a cut
>   Inna yuh barefoot!
> Yuh cyaan walk
>   Inna yuh barefoot!
> So step cool
>   Inna yuh barefoot!
> Doan ac' fool
>   Inna yuh barefoot!

2. Use the words below from the poem to make as many new compound words as you can. Use a dictionary to help you. Here is one to help you.

toe — _toenail, tiptoe, toehold, toecap_

cut — _____

walk — _____

fool — _____

foot — _____ _____

bare — _____

3. Now use some or all of the words in this list to make as many compound words as you can find (there are at least 12). You can use each word more than once. Write your words on the back of this sheet.

head	mouth	eye	ear
hair	tooth	neck	hand
back	foot	drum	ball
sight	light	band	net
brush	grip	ache	lace
bag	book	stand	shake
bone	ground	side	yard
bridge	path	step	man
print	pack		

4. Using a dictionary, check that the compounds you made are real words. Choose five words from your list and write a definition for each one.

Suffixes

CHAPTER FIVE

Intended learning

▶ To recognise and spell common suffixes and understand how these influence word meaning, for example 'ly', 'ful' or 'less'.

▶ To use knowledge of suffixes to generate new words from root words, for example 'proud'/'proudly'.

▶ To begin to use the term 'suffix'.

Starting point: whole class

Working with the text

▶ Explain to the class that they are going to find out about suffixes to help them develop their spelling and vocabulary skills. Discuss the meaning of the term 'suffix'.

▶ Write some examples on the board, such as 'ly', 'ment', 'ful', 'ness', 'fully', 'less', 'est', 'able', 'hood' and 'ship'. Can the children suggest any words that have these suffixes? Write them on the board. Tell them that you would now like them to find some words with suffixes in a story.

▶ Share the text 'The Wind and the Sun'. Ask them to tell you what kind of story it is. Have they heard of this fable before? What message is it trying to tell us?

Working with words

▶ What words in the story can the children find that have a suffix? Underline them and write them on the board with the root word in one colour and the suffix in another. Tell them that many words, such as 'tight', can have several different suffixes attached to them (tightly, tightness, tightest). Explain that a suffix added to a word doesn't necessarily change the meaning of the word but makes the root word fit the way we want to use it in a sentence. For example, words ending in 'ness' are usually abstract nouns used to express someone's feelings or behaviour (happiness/kindness) while words with the suffix 'er' are usually a comparative (strong/stronger) or make a noun (travel/traveller). The suffix 'est' usually indicates a superlative (strong/strongest).

These categories of words are particularly used in fiction and narrative texts where the reader needs to identify with characters and events, such as in the fable in the shared text. Explain that once they know how to spell these suffixes they can generate many more words that will make their own writing more interesting and mature.

▶ Explore this further by asking the children to add suffixes to some root words from the text, such as friend, force and hard.

▶ Discuss some of the rules about suffixes. For example, the silent 'e' at the end of a word is dropped when a vowel suffix is added (hate, hated) but is kept when a consonant suffix is added (hate, hateful) – but remember that there are exceptions (noticeable, argument)!

Group work

Activity sheet 1

This sheet is intended for children who are less-able readers and writers. It requires them to read a simple version of the fable. It concentrates on the suffixes 'ly' and 'ful'.

Activity sheet 2

This sheet is aimed at children who are more confident readers. The tasks are more demanding than on Activity sheet 1 and the text is more complex.

Activity sheet 3

This sheet is aimed at independent readers and writers. The full version of the fable is provided and less support is given.

Plenary session

▶ Consolidate the children's understanding of the term 'suffix' by going over the activity sheet work. Can any of them suggest a definition of the term in their own words? Write it on the board and ask whether the others agree or not.

▶ Discuss any problems they may have had and how they resolved them.

Sentence-level activities

▸ Using the class list of words and/or words generated on the activity sheets, ask the children to make up some sentences, each one incorporating at least one of the suffixed words from the list. They can write them down or just say them. They could try to use as many as possible in one sentence to see what effect this has on the sense (or nonsense) of the sentence. ('You are ruining my happiness with your naughtiness,' Mum shouted angrily and tearfully.)

▸ Provide the children with copies of selected sentences from the text 'The Wind and the Sun'. Mark certain words in the sentences that you want the children to replace. For example, root words, adjectives or adverbs. Ask them to substitute the marked words with words of similar meaning. ('The blue sky quickly reappeared,' might become 'The blue sky rapidly reappeared.') Remind the children to use dictionaries/thesauruses.

▸ Provide sentences from texts where the children are required to complete a cloze procedure task. By omitting root words and/or suffixed words you will again be consolidating their understanding of these.

▸ Using some of the words and sentences from the activity sheets and subsequent work, the children could revise their understanding of adjectives. Ask them to rewrite all or some of the sentences in one of the fables, omitting all the adjectives. What effect does this have? Alternatively they could substitute different adjectives or include as many suitable adjectives as possible into each sentence. Now what is the effect?

Text-level activities

▸ Use the texts 'The Wind and the Sun' and 'Hare and Tortoise' to discuss the concept of a moral. In the first fable the moral is given, but what do the children think is the moral of the second? Look for more stories with morals, such as the rest of Aesop's fables, other traditional tales and the parables of Jesus. What kind of lessons do moral stories teach us? Are they relevant to life today?

▸ Encourage the children to develop their research and note-taking skills by posing some questions for investigation and discussion. For example, comparisons could be made between fables and other types of traditional tales, such as fairy stories, myths and legends. What are the similarities and differences? Are the themes, settings and characters similar? What about stories from other countries; how do they differ? Who was Charles Perrault? (A French writer [1628–1703] who was the first to write down some of the stories with which we are very familiar, including 'Little Red Riding Hood' and 'Sleeping Beauty'.) What country did Aesop come from? Were King Arthur and Robin Hood real people? And so on.

▸ Ask the children to rewrite a fable by giving it a modern setting or by changing the characters.

Fables

The Wind and the Sun

The Wind and the Sun were powerful rivals, always arguing over which of them was the stronger. One day they noticed a man travelling over the hills below them. They decided to settle the argument once and for all by holding a contest to see which of them could get the man's cloak off first. The Wind had the first turn. It blew as hard as it possibly could, sending first one icy blast at the man, then another and another. The man's cloak flapped dreadfully, but he only grasped it all the harder and wrapped himself in it so tightly that the Wind went on vainly blowing until it was completely worn out. It was hopeless!

Then it was the Sun's turn. The Sun sent out its wonderful sunbeams to disperse the black clouds that the Wind had gathered. The blue sky quickly reappeared, and the Sun beamed its hottest rays onto the traveller trudging along below. The man soon began to sweat profusely. He felt so faint with the heat that not only did he fling off his cloak, but also the rest of his clothes, and jumped gratefully into a nearby stream for a refreshing swim. The Sun laughed at the Wind, and said, 'My friend, I have proved that I am stronger than you, and that persuasion is better than force.'

Hare and Tortoise

There was once a hare who was proud and boastful. He liked to brag about how fast he could run to his friend Tortoise, who of course could only go slowly. Hare would often tease Tortoise for being such a slowcoach. But one day, to Hare's surprise, Tortoise suddenly challenged him to a race. Thinking what a funny joke it would be, and that he was certain to win, Hare agreed.

The race began and Hare soon left Tortoise far behind. When he reached the halfway point, Hare decided to stop to rest and play. 'I am so quick that I can easily have a rest,' he said to himself. 'Tortoise is miles behind me.' So Hare settled down in a shady spot for a refreshing nap.

Meanwhile Tortoise plodded on, determined and unresting, straight towards the finish line. 'If I take care and just keep going,' Tortoise said to himself, 'I can win, I hope, and teach Hare a lesson!' In his shady spot, Hare slept longer than he intended. When he woke up, he was surprised to find that Tortoise was nowhere in sight. Off he went again at full speed, but on reaching the finish line, Hare was amazed to see that Tortoise was already there waiting for him! Tortoise was laughing happily, and Hare was very cross indeed!

(Both texts are adapted from *Aesop's Fables*.)

Exploring suffixes

1. Here is another version of Aesop's fable 'Hare and Tortoise'. Read it carefully and then follow the instructions.

Hare was proud of how fast he could run. His friend Tortoise was slow. One day they had a race. Hare soon left Tortoise far behind, so he stopped to rest and play. He thought he was so quick that Tortoise would not catch him. But Hare fell asleep. Meanwhile Tortoise took care to keep plodding on without stopping. When Hare woke up he ran on, but Tortoise was already at the finish line! Tortoise was very happy and Hare was very cross indeed.

2. Add the suffixes 'ly' or 'ful' to these words from the story.

proud _____   friend _____

slow _____   rest _____

play _____   thought _____

quick _____   care _____

cross _____

3. Complete these sentences by making a word with a suffix from the word in brackets. Write the new word in the gap. One has been done for you.

'I can run very fast,' Hare said <u>proudly.</u> (proud)

'I can only go _____' said Tortoise. (slow)

'If I am _____ I can win,' thought Tortoise. (care)

'I will _____ overtake Tortoise,' thought Hare. (easy)

'I'm the winner!' Tortoise shouted _____ (happy)

4. Use the words you have made to write four different sentences on the back of this sheet.

Exploring suffixes

1. Here is part of Aesop's fable 'Hare and Tortoise'.
   Read it carefully and then follow the instructions.

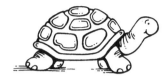

> There was once a hare who was proud and boastful. He liked to brag about how quickly he could run to his friend Tortoise, who of course could only go slowly. One day, to Hare's surprise, Tortoise suddenly challenged him to a race. Thinking what a funny joke it would be, and that he was certain to win, Hare agreed. The race began and Hare soon left Tortoise far behind. When he reached the halfway point, Hare decided to stop to rest and play. 'I am so fast that I can easily have a rest,' he said to himself. 'Tortoise is miles behind me.' So Hare settled down in a shady spot for a refreshing nap.

2. Use a red pencil to circle three words in the story with a suffix (for example, slowly). Write them in these spaces. Write the root words underneath (for example, slow).

   1. _____   2. _____   3. _____

   _____ (root)   _____ (root)   _____ (root)

3. Circle in blue three words in the story that could be root words for suffixes (for example, 'fun' in 'funny'). Find a suffix for each word. Write the new words here (for example, funnily).

   1. _____   2. _____   3. _____

4. Now choose the correct words from the box below to fill in the gaps in these sentences.

   Nicos can _____ say his five times table.

   'I'm _____ at jigsaw puzzles,' said Grandma.

   'Libby is a very kind and _____ girl,' said her teacher.

   'Hare is much too _____,' said Tortoise.

   > playful boastful restful easily certainly hopeless friendly careful

Exploring suffixes

1. You will need a copy of Aesop's fable 'Hare and Tortoise'.
   Read it carefully and then follow the instructions.

2. From the story choose five words that could be root words for suffixes and
   list them below. Then think of at least one suffix for each root and write the
   new words in the spaces. The first one is an example.

   a) proud   proudly   proudest

   b) _____   _____   _____

   c) _____   _____   _____

   d) _____   _____   _____

   e) _____   _____   _____

   f) _____   _____   _____

3. Now list below as many words with suffixes as you can find in the text.

4. On the back of this sheet, write ten new sentences
   using words with suffixes from your lists.

Alphabetical order

Intended learning
- To understand the purpose of alphabetical ordering.
- To organise words or information alphabetically, using the first two letters.

Teacher's note:
You will need a selection of texts containing alphabetically-ordered lists, such as dictionaries, directories and books with indexes.

Starting point: whole class
Working with words
- Tell the children that they are going to do some work on 'alphabetical order'. Discuss what the term means and ask them to think of things that need to be in alphabetical order, such as indexes and dictionaries.
- Provide some books from the collection and ask the children to look through them to consider the following questions. Why is there a need to arrange items alphabetically? Which letter of the alphabet seems to have the most entries? Which has the fewest? Do they notice any rules for the way items are ordered under the individual letters of the alphabet? Discuss how it is easier to find the desired information if you know where and how to look for it.
- Using a dictionary, ask the children how they would find the definitions of words like 'dog' and 'day'. Write the words on the board and ask them to tell you which one they think would come first and why. Explain that alphabetical ordering not only uses the first letter of words but also the second (and sometimes the third, fourth, fifth and so on).
- Show the children how to use the guide words at the top of the dictionary pages to find the correct page. Find the words 'dog' and 'day' in the dictionary and read out the definitions. Repeat this with a different list of words, such as local place-names in a guide.
- Explain that a similar process is used when searching through information books. Show the class some information books with indexes and remind them that the index is

there to help them find information as quickly as possible. Write some of the words from the index on the board and challenge the children to order them alphabetically, and then check that they are right.

Working with the text
- Tell the children that they are going to look at a piece of text taken from an information book about dogs. Share the text and ask what the information is about. Why are certain words underlined? How might this help the reader?
- Their task is to order the underlined words alphabetically as they might appear in an index. Ask them to scan the text to find all the underlined words that begin with 'a' and write them on the board. Continue with each letter of the alphabet. Once the general order is agreed, ask the children to sort the 'a' and 'e' words alphabetically by looking at the second letter in each word.
- Tell the children that they are going to explore alphabetical order further by looking at some more pages from the book about dogs.

Group work
Activity sheet 1
This sheet is for less-able readers and writers. They are asked to sort two different types of list, with support given in the form of clues and an example.

Activity sheet 2
This sheet is for confident readers. They are required to put two lists in alphabetical order but less support is given.

Activity sheet 3
This sheet is a more complex version of Activity sheet 2, aimed at the most-able.

Plenary session
- Share the responses to the activity sheets. Discuss any specific problems the children may have encountered.

Sentence-level activities

▶ Ask the children to make up some alliterative sentences such as 'Adam asked Auntie Anne for an apple.' They could then underline all the words beginning with the same letter and order them alphabetically.

▶ In order to revise and consolidate work on capitals, write lists of names of countries or towns with the initial letters being lower case instead of capitals. This could be presented either as a vertical list or as a sentence with commas. Ask the children to correct the sentence or list.

▶ The children could continue working on dog breeds by exploring adjectives. They could write descriptive sentences about different types of dogs. For example, a sentence about the Border collie might be 'These dogs are intelligent, energetic and easy to train, which makes them ideal for herding sheep.' The completed sentences could be made into a class book with illustrations.

▶ Explore collective nouns by looking at animal examples. A good starting point might be the book *Animal Families* by Colin Threadgall (Julia MacRae books). The children could go on to invent their own collective nouns, for example 'a sting of scorpions'.

Text-level activities

▶ Explore books containing instructional texts. Compare the layout and format of the books. How are the instructions organised? Are diagrams used? How useful are they? Are recipes, for example, easier to follow if they use diagrams and/or illustrations? What good and bad things do the children notice about the instructions? How could they be improved? Challenge the children to write their own set of instructions incorporating all the good points.

▶ Discuss the different ways to obtain information. Consider the advantages and disadvantages of gaining information from a wide range of sources, including comics, radio, television, interviews, listening to a talk, watching a play and chatting to friends. Which is the most effective? Does it depend on who the audience is? Is it easier to remember information if you have watched it on 'Blue Peter' or if you have read it in a magazine? Why? Are school television programmes a better way of learning than reading about the subject in a book? What are the problems with this way of obtaining information? For example, not being able to refer to a television programme again. This activity could take the form of a class or group discussion.

▶ Carry out an information survey. Different groups of children could present the same information to the rest of the class, say on grooming a dog, in different ways. These might include writing a report, writing a set of instructions, drawing a series of diagrams, making a comic strip, producing a cassette tape or video, giving a talk or actually demonstrating with a toy (or real!) dog. Which version was the most interesting and which method enabled them to remember the information best? Why?

▶ Encourage the children to find out more about dogs (or any other animal of their choice). Suggest they choose one or two breeds of dog and use suitable information books to make notes. They could produce information sheets about the breeds.

How to keep a dog healthy

▶ When you own a dog you need to take responsibility for making sure that the dog stays as fit and healthy as possible. There are many things you can do to make sure your dog stays healthy (look up the underlined words in the index for further details).

1 Make yourself aware of the types of <u>ailments</u> a dog can get by buying a book about dog care. Look out for any signs of illness.

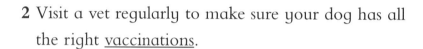

2 Visit a vet regularly to make sure your dog has all the right <u>vaccinations</u>.

3 Don't overfeed your dog. <u>Obesity</u> can make dogs very ill.

4 <u>Exercise</u> your dog every day. Always keep your dog under control when it is out with you.

5 Keep your dog's bedding and <u>food</u> bowls clean.

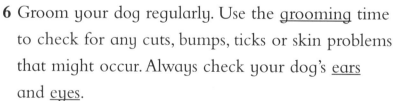

6 Groom your dog regularly. Use the <u>grooming</u> time to check for any cuts, bumps, ticks or skin problems that might occur. Always check your dog's <u>ears</u> and <u>eyes</u>.

7 Keep your dog clean. Make sure it is bathed regularly.

8 Never let your dog roam the streets. Your dog may be involved in an <u>accident</u> or pick up a <u>disease</u>.

Looking after your dog

1. Here is another list from the book about dogs. This one tells you what equipment you need to care for a new dog. Read it carefully. Now write the list in alphabetical order in the spaces below. Use the clues to help you.

collar
identity tag
lead
brush
toys
shampoo
bed
blankets
first-aid kit
bowls
food
treats

be _____
bl _____
bo _____
br _____
co _____
fi _____
fo _____
id _____
le _____
sh _____
to _____
tr _____

2. Below is a list of working dogs. Put them in alphabetical order. The first one has been done for you.

husky, mastiff, collie, lurcher, Newfoundland, sheepdog, spaniel, retriever, terrier.

collie _____   _____   _____

_____   _____   _____

_____   _____   _____

3. How many different types of pet do you know? Make an alphabetical list of them on the back of this sheet.

Looking after your dog

1. Below is part of the index under 'First aid' in the book *Looking After Your Dog*. The publisher forgot to put the list in alphabetical order. Can you sort it out? Write the new list in the box.

Collapse

Shock

Heatstroke

Drowning

Artificial respiration

Burns

Poisoning

Bleeding

Splints

_____

_____

_____

_____

_____

_____

_____

_____

_____

2. Here is another extract from *Looking After Your Dog*. It lists three types of dog breeds. Read it carefully.

Gun dogs	**Hounds**	**Terriers**
cocker spaniel	beagle	Scottish terrier
Weimaraner	Afghan hound	Airedale terrier
golden retriever	basset hound	cairn terrier
springer spaniel	dachshund	Australian terrier

3. In the boxes below rewrite the lists in alphabetical order.

Gun dogs	Hounds	Terriers

4. How many different types of farm animal do you know? List them alphabetically on the back of this sheet.

Looking after your dog

1. Here is part of a list of dog breeds from *Looking After Your Dog*. The publisher has forgotten to put it in alphabetical order. Sort it out and write the new list in the box below.

| dingo |
| Dobermann pinscher |
| Border collie |
| Dalmatian |
| basset hound |
| bearded collie |
| dachshund |
| bloodhound |
| deer-hound |
| bull-terrier |

_____

_____

_____

_____

_____

_____

_____

_____

_____

2. Listed below are some headings for the index from *Looking After Your Dog*. Make up your own index for the book by arranging the headings in alphabetical order in the boxes provided.

Great Dane, feeding, extinct breeds, ears, guard dogs, feet, golden retriever, elderly dogs, foxes, garden safety, eyes, German shepherd, English setter, first aid, guide dogs, exercise, grooming, French bulldog

E	F	G

3. How many types of zoo animal do you know? List alphabetically as many as possible on the back of this sheet.

Antonyms

Intended learning

▶ To explore antonyms, for example upper/lower.

▶ To consolidate dictionary skills and use of definitions.

Starting point: whole class

Working with the text

▶ Explain to the class that this lesson is about 'antonyms' and discuss the meaning of the term. Explain that many opposites can be made by adding a prefix to the word (for, example 'un' + 'easy' = 'uneasy' and 'im' + 'polite' = 'impolite'). Other opposites can be made by adding a suffix to the word, such as 'use', 'useless'. Explain that sometimes antonyms are actually completely different words, for example 'high'/'low' and 'little'/'large'. Ask the children to give you some examples of opposites. Write these on the board and remind them that many thesauruses list antonyms as well as synonyms. Find some words in a thesaurus to demonstrate this.

▶ Tell the children that they are now going to share a story from the Sudan called 'The Coward' to explore antonyms further. Discuss any unfamiliar words and find their definitions in a dictionary. Talk about the text in general – what is the main theme of the story? (The contrast between the cowardly prince and the brave princess.) Can the children pick out any specific words or phrases that emphasise this? Write their suggestions on the board; these might include 'bravest', 'coward', 'cowardice' and 'fear'. Can they think of some opposites for these words? Explain that it is important that the replacement antonym is an appropriate one.

▶ Choose one of the antonyms suggested by the children and use it in the appropriate sentence from the text to illustrate the change of meaning, for example 'He was afraid,' could become 'He was unafraid.'

Working with words

▶ Now cover up all of the story except the first paragraph. Concentrating on this paragraph only, go through the text with the children highlighting any words that could be changed into antonyms. Make sure everyone understands the importance of choosing the best antonym according to the context. Discuss the effect the antonyms have on the text. Do the children think the story will still make sense if this exercise is repeated with every sentence? Will it be more or less interesting/amusing?

▶ Explain that they are now going to look at another part of the story to explore antonyms further.

Group work

Activity sheet 1

This sheet is aimed at children who need greater support. They are provided with a simplified version of the story. They are required to match pairs of opposites, find some of their own antonyms and rewrite some sentences.

Activity sheet 2

Children working on this sheet should be confident readers able to work independently using a dictionary where necessary. They have to find suitable opposites from a wider list of words taken from the extract.

Activity sheet 3

This is aimed at more-able children. They have a longer extract from the story from which to find antonyms. They are required to find definitions and antonyms for six words taken from elsewhere in the story.

Plenary session

▶ Share the activity sheet responses. Does everyone agree that the words selected were the most appropriate? Read through the story again, this time substituting as many antonyms as possible. What is the effect? Is the story better or worse, sensible or ridiculous?

Sentence-level activities

▶ Using adjectives from 'The Coward', such as 'great', 'brave', 'afraid', 'noisy', 'dark' and 'terrible' ask the children to make up two or three sentences describing a real or imaginary scary animal or situation. They should write their descriptions on paper so they can be swapped with a friend. The friend then has to turn the description of the animal or situation into its opposite using appropriate antonyms. Which descriptions are the most vivid or interesting? Why?

▶ Challenge the class to make up crossword puzzles where all the answers are the opposites of the clues.

▶ Look at the punctuation used in the class text. How are the commas used to assist the reader? Where is capitalisation used?

▶ Challenge the class as individuals or pairs to identify all the plurals in 'The Coward'. Can they devise a rule for making plurals? Are there any difficult words that do not obey the rules, for example how does the word 'city' become plural? Are the words 'crowd' and 'enemy' singular or plural? How can they tell? They should transform some of the sentences they identify into the singular form and write them out. Which words in the sentences have they changed? Are there some words that do not have a singular form, such as 'clothes' and 'trousers'?

▶ Ask the children to choose a passage from 'The Coward' and rewrite it omitting any words they think are superfluous to the meaning of the text. What is the effect? Is their version better than the original? Why? Why do they think the author included the words they have deleted?

▶ Discuss whether 'The Coward' is written in the first or third person. How can the children decide this? Suggest that the children imagine they are Samba and challenge them to write letters to his father describing how he found his courage on the battlefield. Would this be in the first or third person?

Text-level activities

▶ Ask the class to write a short diary (four or five entries) of a real or imaginary holiday entitled 'My happy holiday'. They must make everything the opposite of what a reader would expect, for example where everything goes wrong, thus making the holiday an unhappy experience.

▶ Use information leaflets/brochures to provide ideas for changing general meanings as well as individual words. For example, how do Alton Towers and Disneyland sound if the descriptions of the attractions are changed?

▶ Choose a well-known fairy story or nursery rhyme and make it into its opposite, for example, 'The Three Big Pigs'. The children must retell/rewrite the story, while practising opposites and having fun with meanings. Roald Dahl's *Revolting Rhymes* may provide inspiration for this work.

▶ Ask the children to write a sequel to the story of 'The Coward'. Brainstorm ideas as a class. This could be a group or individual activity.

▶ Discuss the characters in the story. Write character portraits of Samba and the princess.

▶ Ask the children to write an alternative ending to 'The Coward'. What would have happened if the princess had not intervened?

▶ Challenge the children to write a guide on 'How to be Brave!' What useful tips can they offer to help others lose their fears?

The Coward (A tale from the Sudan)

A tribe of great warriors had a king who was the bravest man in the world. The king's son, Prince Samba, however, was a coward. He was afraid of everything – the sound of an elephant trumpeting, the roar of a lion, a noisy crowd of people – they all made him run away and hide until the danger was over. He became known throughout the land as Samba the Coward.

When at last he grew tired of his reputation, he ran away in the dark of night to a city where no one knew him. The king of this land had a beautiful daughter, and she fell in love with Samba because, despite his cowardice, he was very handsome. The princess's father allowed the marriage and for some time Samba and his wife lived happily. The people of the city were proud of the young couple who were so attractive and loved each other so much.

Then one terrible day an army from an enemy tribe came and stole all the city's sheep and goats and killed all the shepherds. The warriors from Samba's adopted homeland gathered, calling on Samba to lead them into battle.

'Prince Samba!' they cried. 'Ride at the head of our army and we shall defeat these thieving ruffians!' But of course Samba was nowhere to be found. At last the princess discovered him, hiding in the darkest cellar of the palace and trembling with fear. She could do nothing to make him come out and lead the men. So she dressed herself in Samba's armour, leapt onto his horse and thundered out of the city at the head of the army. Disguised in this way, the princess led the soldiers to an easy victory. When she arrived back at the palace, instead of being angry with Samba she said, 'Quickly put your armour on, and let everyone believe that it was you who defeated the enemy.' So Samba did as the princess said, and received the cheers of the people as if he had won the battle single-handed.

Alas, a few days later the enemy were again at the city gates. Again Samba would not fight, and again the princess rode out at the head of the army disguised in Samba's armour. This time one of the princess's brothers guessed what was happening and in the heat of the battle deliberately wounded her in the leg. Only when the princess returned victorious to her rooms did she see the blood. As Samba was again swapping his clothes for the armour, the princess said, 'Samba, you must give yourself the same wound or the secret of your cowardice will be out, and the people will no longer love you.' 'What!' Samba shrieked in terror. 'Hurt myself? Are you mad?' But before he realised what was happening the princess stabbed his leg. In this way the princess's brother was tricked into believing that Samba had indeed led the army again.

Next day the enemy attacked again. Samba once more refused to fight, but agreed to lead the army out of the city and change armour with the princess in a secret glade. But as soon as Samba sprang into the saddle, the clever princess whipped his horse so hard that it galloped out of the city and across the desert with the soldiers speeding behind and Samba powerless to stop. Soon Samba was in the thick of the battle, surrounded by soldiers and with no escape. It was kill or be killed. Finding his courage at last, he seized his sword and fought as fiercely as anyone could have wished. The enemy were again defeated and fled, never to return.

Samba truly was a hero this time, and was welcomed by the old king and the citizens with shouts and cheers of thanks. Prince Samba turned to his wife, the princess, and said to the king, 'You should thank your daughter and not me, because she has turned me from a coward into a brave man.'

Exploring antonyms

1. Here is part of the story 'The Coward'. Read it carefully.

Samba ran away in the <u>dark</u> of <u>night</u> to a city where no one knew him. The <u>king</u> of this land had a beautiful <u>daughter</u>. She fell in love with Samba because although he was a coward he was also very <u>handsome</u>. The princess's <u>father</u> allowed them to get married. For some time Samba and his wife lived happily. The people of the city were <u>proud</u> of the <u>young</u> couple who loved each other so much.

2. Below on the left are the underlined words from the story and on the right some opposites. They are jumbled up. Match the opposites. The first one has been done for you.

dark   old
night   ugly
king   light
daughter   mother
handsome   ashamed
father   queen
proud   day
young   son

3. Here are some more words from the story. Find opposites for them and write your answers in the spaces provided. The first one shows you how.

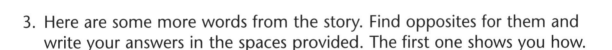

no one   <u>someone</u>
beautiful   _____
love   _____
princess   _____
his   _____
wife   _____
happily   _____

4. Now rewrite two sentences from the extract above using the opposites you have made. Use the back of this sheet for your work.

Exploring antonyms

1. Here is an extract from 'The Coward'. Read it carefully and then follow the instructions.

> Samba was nowhere to be found. At last the princess discovered him, hiding in the darkest cellar of the palace and trembling with fear. She could do nothing to make him come out and lead the men. So she dressed herself in Samba's armour, leapt onto his horse and thundered out of the city at the head of the army. Disguised in this way, the princess led the soldiers to an easy victory.

2. Find a suitable antonym for each of the following words from the text. You can use a thesaurus to help you.

nowhere   somewhere _____

found   _____

darkest   _____

cellar   _____

nothing   _____

out   _____

lead   _____

dressed   _____

head   _____

easy   _____

3. Now choose three sentences from the text above and rewrite them using some of the antonyms you found. Use the back of this sheet for your work.

4. Use a dictionary to find definitions for the words below. Then find a suitable antonym for each one and make up a sentence for each. Write your definitions and sentences on another sheet of paper.

| roar | terrible | arrive | believe | enemy | refuse |

Exploring antonyms

1. Here is an extract from 'The Coward'. Read it carefully and then follow the instructions.

> Next day the enemy attacked again. Samba once more refused to fight, but agreed to lead the army <u>out of</u> the city and change armour with the princess in a secret glade. But as soon as Samba sprang into the saddle, the clever princess whipped his horse so hard that it galloped out of the city and across the desert with the soldiers speeding behind and Samba powerless to stop. Soon Samba was in the thick of the battle, surrounded by soldiers and with no escape. It was kill or be killed. Finding his courage at last, he seized his sword and fought as fiercely as anyone could have wished. The enemy were again defeated and fled, never to return.

2. Underline at least nine words or phrases in the text that could be changed to their opposites. List them below. Then find an antonym for each word or phrase and add these to your list. Use a thesaurus to help you. One has been done for you.

word or phrase	antonym
out of	into
_____	_____
_____	_____
_____	_____
_____	_____
_____	_____
_____	_____
_____	_____
_____	_____

3. Now choose three sentences from the text above and rewrite them using some of the antonyms you found. Use the back of this sheet.

4. Use a dictionary to find definitions for the words below. Then find a suitable antonym for each one and make up a sentence for each. Write your definitions and sentences on another sheet of paper.

warrior	receive	few	deliberately	victorious	welcomed

Common expressions

Intended learning

▶ To be able to recognise common ways of expressing surprise, apology, greeting, warning, thanking, refusing and so on, using letters as a stimulus.

▶ To start collecting, investigating and classifying common expressions in letters and own reading and experience, and use them appropriately.

Starting point: whole class

Working with words

▶ Initiate a discussion on common expressions by asking the children to think of the different ways people greet each other. List these on the board. These might include 'Good morning', 'Hello', 'Hi', 'Nice to meet you', 'How do you do?', 'How are you?' and 'Good evening'. Do the same with expressions of farewell. Are the children aware that greetings/farewells are different across the world? What do local people say? What do people say from other areas?

▶ Consider the different formal and informal situations in which people use these expressions, for example in the street, on the phone, in letters, addressing a group and one-to-one. Discuss which greetings and farewells from the list on the board would be appropriate in different situations, such as chatting to a friend in the playground and writing a holiday postcard to Granny.

▶ Tell the children that they are also going to consider ways of expressing thanks, surprise, congratulations and regret. Say that one way people do this is by writing letters and cards to each other. Brainstorm when people write letters or cards.

Working with the text

▶ Tell the children that they are going to share a letter written by a teacher thanking a zoo-keeper for talking to the children on a school visit. Explain that the letter contains some words and phrases that are common expressions of thanks, regret and surprise. Challenge them to find these as you share the letter.

▶ What words were used to express thanks? Write these on the board. What other words/phrases can the children think of to express thanks? For example, 'Thank you very much', 'I'm thankful', 'thankfulness', 'I'm pleased/glad/obliged', 'with gratitude', 'I appreciate', 'Three cheers for' or 'A round of applause for'. Add these to the list on the board. Do the same exercise for expressions of regret and surprise.

▶ Try substituting some of the words and expressions in the letter with other words/phrases to see what effect this has. Do the children think the new expressions are better than the original ones? Why?

▶ Tell the children that they are going to look at some other letters to explore common expressions further. Tell them that the letters were written by some of the children who went on the safari park trip.

Group work

Activity sheet 1
This sheet is aimed at children who need some support.

Activity sheet 2
Children working on this sheet should be confident readers able to work independently using a dictionary where necessary.

Activity sheet 3
This sheet is aimed at more-able children.

Plenary session

▶ Review the activity sheet work with the whole class. Discuss the meanings of any unfamiliar words. Did they all recognise the expressions in their letters? Were they able to classify the lists of expressions correctly? Did they have any problems? Were any of the expressions on the activity sheets new to them?

Sentence-level activities

▶ Ask the children to make up phrases or sentences for notices containing common expressions for certain situations, such as to warn someone of deep water in a canal – for example 'Danger! Deep water'.

▶ Common expressions for various situations can be made into a classification game. Write some expressions on individual cards, with six expressions for six categories, such as farewell, greeting, thanks, refusal, agreement and warning. Each player has one of the large 'category cards' each. The playing cards are shuffled, dealt out, traded and collected in the way of 'Happy Families'. Each time someone gets a new card they have to say a sentence containing that expression. The first player to fill their category wins.

▶ Use extracts from some of the letters as a starting point for exploring pronouns, distinguishing the 1st, 2nd and 3rd person forms. Challenge the children to rewrite the letters from a different person, for example the brother of someone in the class. How would this alter the pronouns used?

Text-level activities

▶ Ask the children to write their own versions of the letters about the trip to the African Experience Safari Park. They can use ideas from the activity sheets, or write about a real visit they have made to a similar place. The letter should be set out properly with the address of their home or school, the date and so on. They could include some descriptions about the animals they saw, the parts they enjoyed most and some common expressions where possible.

▶ Ask the children to collect unwanted items of mail from home. These might be postcards, circulars and other junk mail, appointment reminders, brochures, thank you letters, bills, greetings cards, advertising and so on. Challenge groups of children to sort the mail into categories, recording how they decide on the categories and which items fall into them. Use this work as a stimulus to discuss the purpose of mail.

▶ Use publicity brochures from a local wildlife centre as a basis for the children designing their own leaflets about an imaginary zoo or wildlife park. What essential information should be included? What other information should be given to make the place seem attractive? What illustrations will be used?

▶ Challenge the class to write exactly 20 words describing a visit they have made to a place of interest. They must have the exact number of words specified. Discuss the conventions of postcard writing. The children could then make their own postcards.

▶ Ask the children to find out what happens to a letter once it has been posted. Investigate the postal service using books, the Internet, videos and so on. Make a class book of their research.

Main Street School
Hightown
Boroughshire
HT1 4BP

Claire Jones
Head Keeper
African Experience Safari Park
Middleton
MD6 9AA

21st September 2001

Dear Ms Jones,

I am very grateful to you for helping us have such an exciting and interesting trip to the African Experience Safari Park yesterday. We really enjoyed the talk you gave on the great apes and the class has decided to raise some money to sponsor a gorilla. One of the highlights for Class 3 was seeing Zazu the baby chimp being hand-reared by your team of keepers. The children were astonished by some of the tricks he got up to and are hoping to return to see him again when he is older.

We also enjoyed the boat trip around the lake. The children thought it was hilarious when the hippopotamus suddenly appeared right by the side of the boat! I am sorry there was so much screaming, but I think they were worried the boat was going to sink!

Thank you once again for making our day so successful. We learned a great deal that will help with our class project on endangered species. I am enclosing some letters written by the children. I hope you enjoy reading them.

Yours sincerely,

Susan Miller
Teacher, Class 3

Common expressions

1. Here is Joshua's letter to the head keeper. Read it carefully.

21st September 2001   Class 3

Dear Ms Jones,

I had a super time at the safari park. Thank you very much for showing us the animals. My favourites were the apes. I liked the gorillas and chimpanzees best, but it was a shock when they suddenly started screaming! Zazu was great, especially the bit where he was having his bottle and then took off his keeper's glasses. I've asked my dad to bring me back to see Zazu again.

Best wishes from
Joshua Bentwood

2. In Joshua's letter underline in blue an expression that shows he is thankful to have visited the safari park. Then underline in red an expression that shows he had a surprise.

3. Sort these expressions into the correct boxes.

| Suddenly | | Thank you very much | | Well I never! |

| Goodness gracious me! | | I'm grateful | | Thank goodness for that! |

Surprise	**Thanks**

4. Now think of one more expression for each box. Make up a sentence for each one and write them on the back of this sheet.

Common expressions

1. Here is Caroline's letter to the head keeper. Read it carefully.

21st September 2001   Class 3

Dear Ms Jones,

I really enjoyed our trip to the African Experience Safari Park. Thank you very much for your talk. My favourite part was the ride around the wildlife park in the bus painted with zebra stripes. It was exciting when three lion cubs suddenly came right up to the bus with the mother lioness! I was sorry when they ran off so quickly. Another bit I liked was seeing the giraffes' heads sticking up above the treetops. Then one went galloping off when the bus got closer. It was an interesting day and all the animals were fantastic.

Best wishes from
Caroline Shawcross

2. In Caroline's letter underline in blue an expression that shows she is thankful. Underline in red an expression that shows she had a surprise. Underline in pencil an expression that shows she regrets something.

3. Now sort these expressions into the correct boxes.

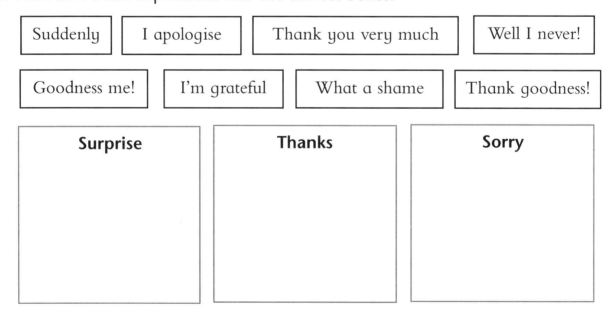

| Suddenly | I apologise | Thank you very much | Well I never! |

| Goodness me! | I'm grateful | What a shame | Thank goodness! |

Surprise	**Thanks**	**Sorry**

4. Now think of one more expression for each box and make up a sentence for each one. Write them on the back of this sheet.

Common expressions

1. Here is Alexander's letter to the head keeper. Read it carefully.

21st September 2001   Class 3

Dear Ms Jones,

Thank you so much for making our trip to the African Experience Safari Park so interesting. I found out a lot of information about the animals we saw. I enjoyed it all, but one of my favourite bits was the Parrot Party. The parakeets and cockatoos were very clever riding their bikes and doing skateboard tricks. I jumped out of my skin when Clarence the cockatoo flew onto my head! Mrs Miller took a photograph of it. I also enjoyed seeing the new penguin enclosure with the artificial iceberg. I thought the macaroni penguins were very cute with the funny feathery bits behind their ears. I was sorry we had to leave.

Thanks again and best wishes from
Alexander MacDonald

2. In Alexander's letter circle an expression that shows he is thankful, one that shows he had a surprise, and one that shows he regrets something.

3. Sort these expressions into the correct boxes.

   All of a sudden – Thankfully – Forgive me – Unexpectedly – Regrettably
   Good heavens! – With gratitude – Ta very much – Pardon me

Surprise	Thanks	Sorry

4. Now think of one more expression for each box. Choose two expressions from each box and make up a sentence for each one. Write them on the back of this sheet.

Synonyms

Intended learning

▶ To collect synonyms that will be useful in writing dialogue, for example 'shouted', 'cried' and 'yelled', exploring the effects on meaning, through substituting these synonyms in sentences.

Starting point: whole class

Working with words

▶ Explain to the class that this lesson is about synonyms and ask them to remind you what they are. Look up the definition in a dictionary. Can they give an example?

▶ Ask them to consider the word 'big' and see how many synonyms they can suggest for it. Write sentences on the board, such as 'Sophie often fights with her **big** sister', 'You need a **big** voice to read a story to the class' and 'It was Ranjit's **big** day'. Discuss what the word 'big' means in each one.

▶ Show the children how to use a thesaurus to find words of similar meaning. They should begin to see that a simple word like 'big' has many possible meanings and that sometimes it is better to choose an alternative word to one that could mean so many different things. Discuss why. You could include the following points: the writer's intended meaning will be clearer for the reader; some words like 'big', 'little', 'nice' and 'said' are over-used and therefore the text will be more interesting to read if alternatives are found; the text will have more impact and hold the reader's attention; it shows a well-developed vocabulary and a more mature style of writing.

▶ Repeat the above with a dialogue word such as 'asked', making sure that everyone also understands what 'dialogue' means.

Working with the text

▶ Tell the children that they are going to read part of a humorous rhyme, 'Jack and the beanstalk', written by Roald Dahl.

▶ Share the text and ask the children to tell you the dialogue words used. Underline the words in the text ('cried', 'yelled' and so on) and list them on the board. Discuss the

effect these words have. What mood do they convey? Is the dialogue loud or quiet? How can you tell? Are the speakers happy, sad, angry, or frightened? What difference would it make if the word 'said' was used every time? Do they think 'cried' is used too much? Can they think of any more words that convey the same mood as 'cried', 'yelled' and so on? A thesaurus can be used to help. Add these new words to the list.

▶ Now explore how changing the dialogue words can have an effect on meaning. For example, 'The mother said, "You lunatic!"' can become 'The mother whispered', 'The mother screamed' or 'The mother taunted'. Discuss how the word used affects the way the reader reads the sentence and interprets the meaning. Repeat this activity with other sentences.

Group work

Activity sheet 1

This sheet is for children who need support. They have to identify two words suggesting loud dialogue, choose four synonyms from a list of suggestions and complete two sentences.

Activity sheet 2

Children working on this sheet should be able to work independently. They are required to identify words suggesting loud dialogue in their extract, select synonyms from a suggested list and complete four sentences.

Activity sheet 3

This is aimed at more-able children. They have a longer extract and are required to complete more complex tasks.

Plenary session

▶ Revise the children's understanding of the terms 'synonym' and 'dialogue'. Discuss the activity sheets and compare the synonyms the children chose. Did they think some of the synonyms were more suitable than others? Why?

Sentence-level activities

▶ Using parts of the Roald Dahl extracts, consider individual sentences. Does the fact that the story is written in rhyme affect the way the sentences are constructed? Is the punctuation different (for example, capital letter at the start of each line)? If it was an ordinary story, might the words be in a different order? If so, why? Are there any other differences?

▶ Use sentences from the extracts for pronoun practice. One way is to remove the pronouns from the sentences for the children to fill in, such as 'The Giant's eaten up ____ mum! ____ smelled _____ out! _____'s in _____ belly!'

▶ Carry out similar work to the above but concentrating on the punctuation used for dialogue. Provide sentences such as 'Cindy shouted let me go' and 'She said my dear are you all right'. Ask the children to produce correctly punctuated versions. They could go on to write their own dialogue to be acted out.

▶ What is the narrative voice in the Dahl extracts – are they written in the first or third person? How can you tell? What would be different if they were written in the first person? What effect would this have? Ask the children to change some sentences from first to third person and vice versa to consolidate their understanding and skills.

Text-level activities

▶ Use the Dahl extracts as a stimulus for the children to retell their own versions of 'Cinderella' and 'Jack and the Beanstalk'. They could either start off the stories and finish with the extracts or continue from the extracts to the end. They should include as many different dialogue words as possible.

▶ Look at the rest of the rhymes in *Revolting Rhymes* by Roald Dahl and compare his versions of stories with other versions the children know. What changes to the plot has Dahl made from the more traditional versions? How have the characters changed, if at all? What is the overall effect of writing the stories in rhyme?

▶ Explore other humorous poems. Make a class collection. Compare different types of humour. Which poems do they find particularly funny? Why?

▶ Use the class text as a stimulus for investigating how words and phrases can signal the passage of time. Consider the sequence Dahl has used (when … then … at ten p.m. … by morning …) to show how the events fit into the time-scale of the story. By looking at prose stories as well, challenge the children to find other examples. These could be collected for future reference when the class are writing their own stories.

▶ Use *Revolting Rhymes* as a stimulus for looking at other fiction by Roald Dahl. What other titles by Dahl do the children already know? Have they read these? Can they say anything about his style of writing? If they like his books, can they say why? The discussion could also include the idea of sequels and continuing themes, characters and so on, as in *Charlie and the Chocolate Factory* and *Charlie and the Great Glass Elevator*.

Jack and the beanstalk

When Jack produced one lousy bean,
His startled mother, turning green,
Leaped high up in the air and cried,
'I'm absolutely stupefied!
'You crazy boy! D'you really mean
'You sold our Daisy for a bean?'
She snatched the bean. She yelled, 'You chump!'
And flung it on the rubbish-dump.
Then summoning up all her power,
She beat the boy for half an hour,
Using (and nothing could be meaner)
The handle of a vacuum-cleaner.
At ten p.m. or thereabout,
The little bean began to sprout.
By morning it had grown so tall
You couldn't see the top at all.
Young Jack cried, 'Mum, admit it now!
'It's better than a rotten cow!'
The mother said, 'You lunatic!
'Where are the beans that I can pick?
'There's not one bean! It's bare as bare!'
'No no!' cried Jack. 'You look up there!
'Look very high and you'll behold
'Each single leaf is solid gold!'

From *Revolting Rhymes* by Roald Dahl

Dialogue synonyms

1. Read this extract from 'Cinderella' by Roald Dahl.

She bellowed 'Help!' and 'Let me out!'
The Magic Fairy heard her shout.
Appearing in a blaze of light,
She said, 'My dear, are you all right?'
'All right?' cried Cindy. 'Can't you see
'I feel as rotten as can be!'
She beat her fist against the wall,
And shouted, 'Get me to the Ball!'

2. In the extract Cinderella is speaking loudly. Underline two words in the text that show this. Write the words here.

1. _____   2. _____

3. From the list below, choose four words that could be used instead of the words you underlined. Write them below.

yelled whispered bawled shrieked sobbed roared asked snarled screamed

a) _____   c) _____

b) _____   d) _____

4. Complete these sentences using a synonym for the word in brackets. Choose words from the list above. The first one has been done for you.

'Can you find me a pumpkin?' the Magic Fairy _____asked_____.(enquired)

'I'll never go to the ball,' Cinderella _____ (cried)

'Let me try on the slipper!' the Ugly Sister _____ (yelled)

Dialogue synonyms

1. Read this extract from 'Cinderella' by Roald Dahl.

He grabbed her dress to hold her back.
As Cindy shouted, 'Let me go!'
The dress was ripped from head to toe.
She ran out in her underwear,
And lost one slipper on the stair.
The Prince was on it like a dart,
He pressed it to his pounding heart,
'The girl this slipper fits,' he cried,
'Tomorrow morn shall be my bride!'

2. In the extract are two dialogue words showing that Cinderella and the Prince are talking loudly. Underline them.

3. From the list below, choose four synonyms that could be used instead of the words you underlined. Write them below.

   yelled   whispered   bawled   shrieked   sobbed   roared   asked

   snarled   declared   murmured   screamed   squealed   enquired

   bellowed   muttered   announced

   a) _____   c) _____

   b) _____   d) _____

4. Now complete these sentences using a synonym for the word in the brackets. The list above might help you.

   'Let me go!' Cinderella _____ (shouted)

   'I shall marry whoever this slipper fits!' Prince Charming _____ (said)

   'Let me try on the slipper!' the Ugly Sister _____ (shrieked)

   'Thank you, Fairy Godmother,' Cinderella _____ (murmured)

Dialogue synonyms

1. Read this extract from 'Jack and the beanstalk' by Roald Dahl.

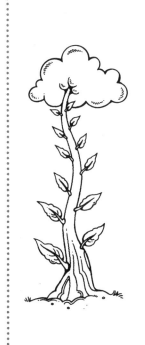

From somewhere high above the ground
There came a frightful crunching sound.
He heard the Giant mutter twice,
'By gosh, that tasted very nice.
'Although (and this in grumpy tones)
'I wish there weren't so many bones.'
'By Christopher!' Jack cried. 'By gum!
'The Giant's eaten up my mum!
'He smelled her out! She's in his belly!
'I had a hunch that she was smelly.'
Jack stood there gazing longingly
Upon the huge and golden tree.
He murmured softly, 'Golly-gosh,
'I guess I'll have to take a wash
'If I am going to climb this tree
'Without the Giant smelling me.'

2. Find dialogue words that show that Jack and the Giant speak quietly and one that shows Jack also speaks loudly. Underline them.

3. Now find three synonyms that could be used instead of the words you underlined. Think of your own or use the list below.

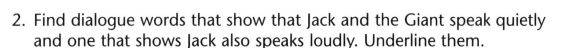

4. Now choose a synonym for each word in brackets to finish these sentences. The list below might help you.

'You swapped Daisy for one bean?' Jack's mum _____ (enquired)

'Yes, but it's a magic bean,' Jack _____ (responded)

'Fee fi fo fum, I smell the blood of an Englishman!' the Giant _____ (shouted)

exclaimed laughed replied asked screamed breathed bawled
grinned roared whispered answered questioned bellowed
queried yelled muttered argued giggled hissed

Homonyms

Intended learning

- To be able to recognise that some words with the same spelling or pronunciation have more than one meaning and that these words are called homonyms.
- To understand that the intended meaning of homonyms is distinguished by examining the context.
- To identify and use homonyms.

Starting point: whole class

Working with the text

- Tell the children that they are going to do some work exploring homonyms. Do they know what homonyms are? Explain that they are words that have more than one meaning but are spelled or pronounced the same. Write the word 'wave' on the board as an example. Challenge them to think of as many meanings for it as possible. These may include a wave of the hand, a wave in the sea, a wave shape, a kink in the hair, to move backwards and forwards, to flutter and so on. Then ask 'When we see the word 'wave' in a sentence how do we know which meaning is intended?' Discuss this idea, emphasising the importance of context in interpreting meanings. Write sentence examples on the board.
- Share the class text 'Foolish questions'. Explain that the poem contains some more homonyms. Discuss the poem. Do the children like it? Why/why not? What do they notice about the words used? Is the poet having fun with words? Why do they think the poet gave the poem its title?

Working with words

- How many words can the children find that are homonyms? Share the different meanings of some of the words, for example 'cap' and 'nails'. Remind them that dictionaries can be used to find all the different meanings and ask them to look up some of the words. How many different meanings are listed for 'cap', for example?

Challenge them to use some of these words in sentences to show the different meanings. Emphasise how looking at the word in context tells us which meaning of the word is intended.

- Discuss how homonyms can be used to create humour in everyday language through the use of puns.
- Explain that they are going to explore the use of homonyms further.

Group work

Activity sheet 1

This sheet is aimed at children who need more support. They are asked to complete several sentences using the words 'fly', 'fish' or 'course'. They are then asked to match words to their meanings, using a dictionary for support and to write their own sentences.

Activity sheet 2

Children working on this sheet should be confident readers able to work independently. They are required to complete sentences using the words 'felt', 'piece' and 'same'. They then have to find two different definitions for four words and write their own sentences.

Activity sheet 3

This is aimed at more-able readers with a wider vocabulary. They have to use six different words when completing their sentences. They then use a dictionary to find as many different meanings as they can for another six words. They are also required to use these words in sentences.

Plenary session

- Revise the children's understanding of the term 'homonym'. Ask some of them to read out some sentences from their activity sheets to check that they have inserted the correct homonym. Did they manage to find different definitions for the listed words? Were there any specific difficulties? Compare the definitions the children came up with. Which word did they find the most meanings for?

Sentence-level activities

▶ Discuss the punctuation in the poem. For example, why do some lines end with a comma, question mark or a full stop? Why does each line start with a capital letter even if it is not the start of a new sentence? The difference between prose and poetry layout could be investigated, for example what happens to the layout and punctuation when the poem is rewritten as prose?

▶ The poem uses lots of questions. Can the children think of suitable answers for each one? Explore the different types of questions used, such as where, what, who, how and can. Challenge them to turn statements into questions beginning with these words.

▶ Use the body parts mentioned in the poem to explore singular and plural. One eye, two eyes, one calf, two calves and so on.

▶ Use the poem 'Foolish questions' as a stimulus for investigating personal and possessive pronouns. The children could mark all the personal pronouns (I, he, you) in one colour and the possessive ones in another. What other possessive pronouns are there? How would the poem change if the first line was 'Where can a woman buy a cap for her knee?'

▶ Ask the children to choose a piece of writing they have already produced in a previous lesson. They should reproduce it, this time substituting pronouns for common and proper nouns. What effect does this have? Is the meaning clear?

▶ Challenge the children to make 'Foolish questions' into a dialogue between two, or more, people. They will have to decide where to divide the poem and rewrite it as a conversation using speech marks and other dialogue punctuation. This could be done in pairs, with each pair recording their conversation onto tape.

Text-level activities

▶ What makes this poem funny? Do the children enjoy humorous poems? Explore other forms of humorous verse, such as jokes, word games, calligrams, shape poems and limericks. Make a class book of found/children's own poems.

▶ Challenge them to write a similar poem using words that can have two meanings. They could also invent fantasy responses to the questions in the poem. For example, a labelled diagram of a machine designed to sharpen shoulder blades, a 'wanted' poster for the crook of an elbow or a detailed description of the jewels that can be found in the crown of a head.

▶ Explore other poems written about the body. How many different kinds can they find? Make a class collection.

▶ Make a class book of questions and answers. The children could work in pairs. Each child writes a question and gives it to their partner to find out or invent an answer to it. The book could be about fantasy questions and replies or serious questions about the current class topic.

▶ Ask the class to use reference materials or the Internet to find out about the human body. They could word-process their findings and put the information into an alphabetically-ordered book.

Foolish questions

Where can a man buy a cap for his knee?

Or a key for the lock of his hair?

And can his eyes be called at school?

I would think – there are pupils there.

What jewels are found in the crown of his head,

And who walks on the bridge of his nose?

Can he use, in building the roof of his mouth,

The nails on the ends of his toes?

Can the crook of his elbow be sent to jail –

If it can, well, then what did it do?

And how does he sharpen his shoulder blades?

I'll be hanged if I know – do you?

Can he sit in the shade of the palm of his hand,

And beat time with the drum of his ear?

Can the calf of his leg eat the corn on his toe? –

There's somethin' pretty strange around here!

American Folk Rhyme adapted by William Cole

Homonyms

1. Read through this poem. Find and underline the homonyms.

> **I wonder why?**
>
> Did the fly fly by?
> I wonder why?
> To see the fish fish
> Of course!

2. Use underlined words from the poem to complete these sentences.

   The humming-bird is the only bird able to _____ backwards.

   The trout is a type of _____

   We watched my dad play on the golf _____

   My dog had to have a _____ of injections.

   I tried to _____ my book out of the bottom of my bag.

   The _____ settled on top of the food.

3. Match these words to their meanings. Each word has two different meanings. Use a dictionary to help you.

match	to stumble
	to make a sound like a bell
ring	a sporting game where teams play
	a short journey
trip	a round band worn on the finger
	a small stick with a special tip that can make a flame

4. On the back of this sheet, write two sentences for each word to show the different meanings.

Homonyms

1. Read this poem. Find and underline the homonyms.

> **Of all the…**
>
> Of all the felt I ever felt,
> I never felt a piece of felt
> That felt the same as that felt felt,
> When I first felt that felt.

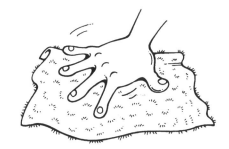

2. Use underlined words from the poem to complete these sentences.

We used coloured _____ to make a collage.

Whether we go to the park or the zoo, it's all the _____ to me.

I didn't know how he _____ about going to the cinema.

He spent a ten pence_____ on a packet of sweets.

She is wearing the _____ shirt as last time.

We all had a _____ of cake each.

3. Find two definitions for each of the words below. Use a dictionary to help
   you. On the back of this sheet, write a sentence to go with each definition.

   ring   match   watch   duck

_____

_____

_____

_____

_____

_____

_____

_____

Homonyms

1. Read this poem. Find and underline the homonyms.

> ### Doctor Bell
>
> Doctor Bell fell down a well
> And broke his collar-bone.
> Doctors should attend the sick
> And leave the well alone.

2. Use underlined words from the poem to complete these sentences.

We are going to _____ a wedding next week.

The soldier was home on _____

The forester had to _____ four old trees.

The boy couldn't play football because he was _____

'Mum, please tell him to _____ me alone!'

'I am _____ and tired of hearing you say that!' she said.

I hope you will be _____ enough to visit us next week.

Mary tripped over and _____ the good vase.

My brother is a keen _____ walker.

Can you _____ to the garden for me?

My little sister always gets car _____

3. Find as many definitions as you can for the words below. Use a dictionary to help you. Make up a sentence to go with each definition and write them on the back of this sheet.

watch   light   set   rule   type   dash

Acknowledgements

The author and publisher gratefully
acknowledge permission to reproduce copyright
material in this book.

'The Bogeyman' by Jack Prelutsky from
Nightmares: Poems to Trouble Your Sleep,
published by A&C Black , 1976

'Jack and the Beanstalk' and 'Cinderella from
Revolting Rhymes by Roald Dahl, published by
Jonathan Cape.

'Barefoot' by Martin Glynn. Permission kindly
granted by the poet.

'Sasquatch', 'Nessie' and 'Yeti' are all from the
poem 'Three of a kind' by Richard Edwards.
Grateful thanks to the author for permission
to reproduce.